T0124325

# Awaken

*A Personal Journey of Enlightenment*

## Jin Nua

**BALBOA**.
PRESS

A DIVISION OF HAY HOUSE

Copyright © 2015 Jin Nua.

All rights reserved. No part of this book may be used or reproduced by
any means, graphic, electronic, or mechanical, including photocopying,
recording, taping or by any information storage retrieval system
without the written permission of the publisher except in the case
of brief quotations embodied in critical articles and reviews.

Balboa Press books may be ordered through booksellers or by contacting:

Balboa Press
A Division of Hay House
1663 Liberty Drive
Bloomington, IN 47403
www.balboapress.com
1 (877) 407-4847

Because of the dynamic nature of the Internet, any web addresses or
links contained in this book may have changed since publication and
may no longer be valid. The views expressed in this work are solely those
of the author and do not necessarily reflect the views of the publisher,
and the publisher hereby disclaims any responsibility for them.

The author of this book does not dispense medical advice or prescribe the use
of any technique as a form of treatment for physical, emotional, or medical
problems without the advice of a physician, either directly or indirectly. The
intent of the author is only to offer information of a general nature to help
you in your quest for emotional and spiritual well-being. In the event you use
any of the information in this book for yourself, which is your constitutional
right, the author and the publisher assume no responsibility for your actions.

Any people depicted in stock imagery provided by Thinkstock are
models, and such images are being used for illustrative purposes only.
Certain stock imagery © Thinkstock.

Print information available on the last page.

ISBN: 978-1-5043-3686-4 (sc)
ISBN: 978-1-5043-3687-1 (e)

Library of Congress Control Number: 2015911318

Balboa Press rev. date: 09/29/2015

To Oprah

# Contents

Bodhi is a Theravada term. It literally means "awakening" and "understanding." Someone who is awakened has . gained insight into the workings of the mind which keeps us imprisoned in craving, suffering and rebirth.

—Merriam-webster.com (April 25, 2007)

Looking into one's nature or the opening of satori.

—D. T. Suzuki

A thunderclap under the clear blue sky
All beings on earth open their eyes;
Everything under heaven bows together;
Mount Sumeru leaps up and dances.

—Gatsurin Shikan

*Bodhi* (Sanskrit, Pāli), literally means "to have woken up and understood."

— Ingrid Fischer-Schreiber, Franz-Karl Ehrhard, Michael S. Diener[1]

*Prajna* refers to the particular form of understanding or knowledge that the Buddha attained upon his awakening.

— Sung-Bae Park[2]

Yogacara uses the term *āśraya parāvṛtti*,

"revolution of the basis"

... a sudden revulsion, turning, or re-turning of

the *ālaya vijñāna* back into its original state of

purity ... the mind returns to its original condition of

nonattachment, nondiscrimination, and nonduality.

—Dan Lusthaus[3]


The full enlightenment attributed to Buddha is known

as *samyaksaṃbodhi* (Sanskrit; Pāli: *sammāsaṃbodhi*) or

*anuttarā-samyak-saṃbodhi*, "highest perfect awakening."

—Linnart Mäll[4]

# Introduction

*O*ver fifteen years ago, I experienced a powerful transformation. In many ways, I was awakened. It occurred over the course of a few weeks when a series of close encounters with nature caused a budding awareness of my surroundings to surge in a crescendo, sparking a powerful epiphany that forever changed how I would view the world.

Everything changed—the vividness of colors, the intensity of experience, and my conceptions of man and nature. I gained a seeming freedom to explore all things from any angle without restraints from past beliefs or convictions.

It was a classic "bottom falling out of the bucket" or "becoming aware" event whereby everything suddenly came into sharper focus, innocence reemerged, and deeper understandings took hold. It was as though I'd fallen into a new world—a new terrain filled with wonder, bliss, and awe seemingly only roamed by artists, sages, and monks.

Over the years, I sought to better understand what had occurred. I read books on neurology and philosophy, as well as writings on Buddhist enlightenment, but a suitable explanation remained elusive.

I wondered: Did my mind change? Did an angel-like spirit enter me? Had I tapped into some kind of universal source—a well of knowledge buried beneath the level of reality we experience in our day-to-day existence?

Years later, I came to the somewhat surprising realization that nothing much had really changed. I was still fully myself, complete with my memories, identity, and a full set of emotions. What I came to realize was startlingly simple yet intensely profound: my inner voice—the gentle narrator quietly guiding my day-to-day life—had never changed. The only difference was that a certain control over this voice had been removed.

My inner voice—always reliable and steady—had become unshackled and was once again free to roam. And roam it did. It was a source of pure universal wonder looking upon a similarly beautiful universe, like looking into a mirror. But now the view was clear—no longer obscured by intervening layers of discouraging thoughts and impulses that served only to keep me anxious and confined within a world where only consumption and getting ahead of others were valued.

Back in charge again, I was free to stop, look, and listen to the world with newfound innocence and wonder. I was drawn to all things beautiful and seemingly closer to the divine. Art, literature, music, and especially nature were the new beacons guiding my thoughts. Wonder of being and mysticism filled all moments in between.

Able to couple my past experiences and knowledge with a renewed innocence and purity of thought, I was able to fly effortlessly to the greatest heights of understanding, knowledge, imagination, and creativity.

I believe this is the universe's greatest gift to us—connecting us to the source and placing us in closer proximity to God's grace. Wouldn't you like to come along for the journey? *Awaken* will help you better understand what this all means and how you might bring its great gift into your life.

# *What Is It?*

*D*eep at the core of each of us resides a boundless heart of gold. Some call it our soul; others believe it is God's voice speaking through us. Whatever name it is given, it is the source of all things—an infinite store of universal energy; a boundless well of immense wonder and greatness; and a pure source, recognizing the goodness and beauty in all things, guiding us to act in a similar fashion.

You'll recognize your heart whenever kind thoughts emerge. She's talking when you experience initial reactions, first impressions, and gut feelings. You also recognize her when you're at your best, being truly sincere and selfless and treating others with grace and compassion.

This is a natural outcome. As the philosophy of Centerpath teaches, our lives are reflections of the universe and its grand design. A key feature of this design is nature's creations are packed with large concentrations of pure energy at their core.

It's no different with you and me. We have a core containing limitless energy and purity. And because we may be the universe's most incredible creation, it's quite possible that we possess its most phenomenal core, filled with the high-order qualities of love, compassion, kindness, and grace. Your heart is ready, willing, and able to spread its bountifulness into its surroundings in the most beautiful ways—if you let it.

# What's Holding Us Back?

*S*o what is holding us back from achieving all we're capable of? It's a complicated question but one we can begin to understand when we revisit the time in our lives when spontaneity began to fade.

Watch your children. In the absence of physical pain (and later the pain associated with not getting what they want), their natural disposition is to be spontaneous and full of wonder. They can play a new game or stare at a toy they love for hours, as though it was the first and most profound object they'd ever seen.

During our preteen years all this begins to change, when socialization begins to take a firmer hold on our developing minds. We are conditioned to act in certain ways and to conform to societal norms or face being disciplined and ostracized.[5]

Simultaneously, we are provided with less and less support toward being an individual and thinking independently. We're placed under increasing pressure to become someone— first to formulate a socially acceptable personality and then to "get a life" (i.e., a career).

Over years (and later decades), a new voice often becomes prominent. The part of our minds that is attuned to the needs of the flock takes control and rules our thoughts. It keeps us relevant, normalized, and increasingly on our guard to defend and promote ourselves in social situations.

After a lifetime of such exposure, our little hearts become buried—overrun and obscured by parts of our minds that seek advantage and can't tolerate the pain of a weakened social posture. The one sure and steady thing in our lives becomes increasingly obscured by the chatter associated with an agenda that won't accept anything less than victory as something of value.

In many ways, our true selves are strangled. But inside, our hearts never leave us. The heart is always present, like a lifelong friend, loyal to the end. You can still recognize her gentle ways.

You can begin to restore this essential bond and increasingly reconnect with your heart. Start by loosening your ties with hard society and its swirling agendas. Find more quiet time for yourself; spend more time in nature or studying new and exciting subjects.

Over time, your ears will reopen to what your heart's loving voice is trying to tell you. Listen to your heart, and allow it to once again become your source of simplicity, spontaneity, spirit, and confidence—a sure and steady center from which you can lead your life.

You can again come to know God's voice speaking to you from the heart of the universe, guiding you toward the divine in all of life's interactions. Join us in her kind and gentle invitation to participate in a heartfelt dialogue with the heavens and the heavenly.

# How It Works

Lao Zhu, Blake, Goethe, Whitman, and Van Gogh— the works of each flew off the canvas as if given an enchanted life all of their own. How were they able to produce such breathtaking works beyond the reach of most of us? What could they see and access that we can't? What's their secret? One potential solution comes from Centerpath and the sacred relationship it describes between centers and their surroundings.

Let's start with what we know. Seers and sages report that intense creativity primarily arises from an ability to silence and purify the mind. From Centerpath, we also know that pure centers generate near-perfect symmetries about them, as well as a host of accompanying beneficial properties. The implications arising from the merging of these two statements implies something very profound.

A silenced mind closely approximates a pure center. It allows incoming stimuli—and indeed our thoughts—to flow directly inward without being rerouted to various cognitive subroutines (i.e., worrying over the past, fretting about the future, or allowing preconceived notions to affect the experience).

A silenced mind creates a smooth and undistorted spherical shape as information flows inward in relatively straight and smooth lines. A larger, symmetrical halo shape is the result! A still mind replicates the universe's geometry of choice, allowing sages and seers to reap the attendant benefits of symmetry, balance, beauty, and unity.

The full 360-degree holism generated by this arrangement allows all stimuli, influences, and associated tender nuances to flow in unhindered from any direction. The net result is a freer, wider-flowing, and more complete creation.

Only through achieving this base condition—quite literally matching the preferred geometry of the universe—can we begin to understand the level of insight, wisdom, and creativity that great artists and sages achieve.

But something's still missing. Even this doesn't fully explain the levels of peace and bliss sages, priests, and monks experience when they are in the zone. Indeed, the universe appears to reward near-perfect symmetry with increased flows of energy. Is it real? Does this really happen?

The next chapter attempts to address this delightful enigma.

# But Why? How?

It brought me to the God center, the vortex where
all chakras converge—perhaps the whirlpool begins at
the spiritual center and all life forms
are based on this premise.
—*Janet Marie Burns*

It isn't fully clear why elevated states of bliss accompany heightened awareness. However, one likely explanation comes from the way in which center-oriented designs interact with the universe at large. Fundamentally, all creations—and indeed the universe itself—share the same underlying center-oriented design[6]. This sharing of form generates a powerful resonating effect, not unlike the phenomenon that occurs when tuning forks of the same frequency are struck and their vibrations become sympathetic. In essence, vibrational energy is fed back and forth from one system to the other.

Extending this analogy to the 'tuning forks' of a silenced mind and the universe itself, we discover the same resonant effects at play. Sharing the same geometric frequency the two interact, funneling additional energy into the silenced mind—ultimately contributing to the elevated state of being and enlightenment reported by meditating sages. It's like water running down a drain; if the funnel is smooth and symmetrical, the flow is faster and more efficient.

In many ways, it's similar to the effects described in the ancient practice of tantra whereby the alignment of successive chakras opens a gate, encouraging larger flows of creative energy to run through them. In terms of Centerpath—when your miniverse matches the frequency of the macroverse, you are rewarded with a greater vibrational flow of energy and bliss.

How do we apply this to our lives? Being a child of the universe, the core of your existence naturally strives to obtain this same geometry by being pure at heart. You felt it as a child, living life simply and with pure motivations, freely and spontaneously interacting with others and the environment, happy and joyful.

Unfortunately, over time, much of this spontaneity evaporated, progressively supplanted by social training intended to develop independent, relevant, and—some might say—fierce citizens. However, this magic can be found once more and resurrected.

How do you align yourself with the great universal geometry and the symmetry it engenders? Simply by allowing all things to flow as closely as possible to how they naturally are. This happens when we live in the here and now, not in the past or future or somewhere else.

These *other* places and times only serve to push, pull, expand, contract, and reroute our direct surroundings (and therefore experience), serving to disrupt the symmetric-seeking aura about you. Of course, it doesn't mean you forget about the past or do not take the future into account, but it does mean you should focus as much energy as practical on the here and now.

Through these practices, you will align your world of sensory data and thoughts in the most perfectly symmetric (i.e., undistorted) form possible. By being centered, you will be in full alignment with the universe's great geometry and feel the rush of wonder, insight, and excitement that naturally attends the experience. You will also tread close to the divine and feel the exhilarating spiritual energy that accompanies such lofty places—a kind of holy grail to strive for in life.

Of course, we can't all be monks—the demands of life and family gratifyingly take much of our time and attention. However, we can put at least shades of nature's perfection to work in our lives. One method is to give your full attention and mindfulness to any task at hand (whether it be a conversation, playing with your child, or cleaning dishes). By doing so, you will have created a beautiful geometry of your own making.

It may be no surprise that when we distort the natural symmetry, we create imbalances, deformations, and ugliness that can propagate into all aspects of our lives. In fact, such distortions are the source of practically all of today's ills—a disturbing malaise caused by man taking much more than he needs and thus creating huge imbalances and destructiveness that distort the very fabric of the universe and leave behind a terrible legacy that will surely be judged harshly by history.

# *My Path*

The human mind once stretched by new ideas
never goes back to its original dimension.
—Oliver Wendall Holmes

*E*ach of our paths to a greater awareness will vary in its details, yet all will share common themes (many of which we examine in the remainder of this book). The events leading up to my transformative experience arose from the confluence of three major events: a career change, various personal struggles I was experiencing, and progressively close encounters with nature.

In the year leading up to my transformation, I quit the company I'd worked for since graduating from college to pursue a new opportunity. This event was more challenging than I had ever imagined it would be. I fretted over many things. *What will happen? Will I succeed? What will others think and say about me?* After all, career has so much to do with who we are. My mini identity crisis was exacerbated by various challenges to what I wanted and valued. I found myself expending considerable energy fighting for things I believed in, against others who wanted something else.

The third element leading to my change involved various close encounters with nature's immensity. Just two months prior to the event, I'd taken my first trip to Yellowstone National Park. During this fateful journey, I witnessed the sheer grandeur of the Milky Way on a clear, moonless night. The sky was completely illuminated in a purple hue caused by innumerable stars shining directly through the atmosphere. I was moved.

Another experience serving to widen my perception was the realization that the park's outline actually marked the boundaries of an ancient caldera. Yellowstone's rich diversity and sheer grandeur were largely resultant from its sitting in the bowels of an ancient volcano that collapsed *into* the earth millions of years ago!

As though to prove the adage that all things happen in threes, my third encounter with nature's immensity was with the universe itself. I had a chance to read about the big bang for the first time and was awestruck by the implication that our entire universe began from a highly condensed state of energy over fourteen billion years ago! Yet another colossal change in my understanding of the cosmos!

# The Event

Shortly after my Yellowstone trip, I relocated to Thailand to take up a new work assignment. Taking up residence on the beach, I began to spend more and more time on my balcony gazing at the sea and sky.

Two or three months into this routine, the transformation occurred. The first indication that something had changed was a subtle shift in how I was viewing nature. I no longer turned a blind eye to her presence as before. I instead began to look directly at her many marvels of creation and wonder how they could be the way they were.

For instance, I wondered why shells on the shore curled up in the same shape as the waves crashing about them. Did the crashing wave somehow affect the development of the shell's shape, or did both result from a consistent set of underlying conditions?

But it wasn't until the day a string of clouds floated by as one, just above the top of the building in which I was staying, that I knew something had truly changed. I remember feeling startled by the sudden realization that the cloud appeared alive. It felt as though I'd stepped into a new world where the larger aliveness of things could be seen. No longer obscured by mounds of predisposed beliefs and conventions, I could now see the great cosmic breath in action—animating and breathing life into the ten thousand things.

It was actually a shade unsettling at first. I wasn't sure if I'd permanently left the world I'd known all my life. However, that uncertainty soon gave way to an increasing feeling of emboldened wonder over the coming days and weeks.

Everything had changed. From that moment forward, my view of what nature, man, and being meant, and how deeply they were intertwined, was overturned. Numerous new avenues of thought and creativity I had never imagined possible opened up immediately. Nothing would ever be the same again.

May your journey be as breathtaking and exhilarating!

# Awakening Is Not for Everyone

Let's face it: the human psyche is delicate and complex. The radical changes associated with becoming aware are not for everyone. However, for those better suited to the journey, it is well worth the potential risks.

Who is more likely to make the shift and more likely to negotiate the other side successfully? I believe that persons with the following qualities have a higher chance of succeeding:

- Those in their mid-thirties to mid-forties (i.e., those who've overcome the hurdles of youth but aren't yet too fixed in their ways).
- Introspective types.
- People who are patient and sensible.

- People who are more open and receptive to others and their ideas.

- Those with a solid parental foundation and an expansive upbringing.

- Those with a positive outlook on life.

This doesn't mean other personality types can't make the change, but it may be more difficult to initially break through and then to cope once on the other side. In either event, if one doesn't make it, that's okay too. The habits described in this book are beneficial to anyone who practices them. You stand to lose nothing even if you fall short of the ultimate goal.

# *The Benefits*

*B*ecoming aware brings with it some very real and tangible benefits. In many ways, it is the universe's greatest gift. Consider the value of the following qualities you stand to gain:

- The world will appear fresh and new.
- You'll feel great bliss from experiencing the world and learning new things.
- Nature will become a limitless source of awe and inspiration.
- You will come to realize that you don't know everything. Surprisingly enough, you'll appreciate this as a strength since it keeps us curious and draws us toward deeper understandings.
- You will come to see and appreciate the interconnectivity of all things.

- Your breadth of experience will expand above and below man's layer of experience (i.e., you will be able to dive down into the hearts of atoms as well as soar across galaxies).

- Your appreciation of great thoughts, art, literature, and music will become tangible and deeply heartfelt.

- Your ability to express thoughts, art, literature, and music will expand tremendously (i.e., your creativity will become limitless).

- Your ability to conceptualize and stitch larger ideas together will increase dramatically.

- Your understanding of yourself and others will increase.

- Spirituality will transform from a marketing slogan to a deeply felt emotion.

- Your proximity to the divine will increase.

# The Challenges

The biggest challenges arising from becoming aware relate to interactions with others. Most won't understand or appreciate your newfound enthusiasm. Talking insatiably of nature's beauty and unconventional ideas doesn't resonate with most, and for some, it can be overwhelming if not downright threatening.

Sure, from time to time your words will find captive audiences, but more often than not, you will be considered an outsider. So proceed gently and be ready for disappointments when trying to connect with others.

The other risk comes from ignoring certain parts of our emotions and psyche. Diverting all your time to exploring deep ideas and art means you'll often put aside social interactions and addressing any feelings that might be accumulating. The result can be a sudden outpouring of pent-up emotions larger in intensity than would normally be the case. With this in mind, you'll need to take regular downtime to catch up with others and to give yourself time to work through any emotions that you haven't addressed in some time.

# Meditate

*A*s we touched on earlier, the act of meditation configures our minds into the shape of the universe's geometry of choice (i.e., a center-oriented pattern). Such an arrangement also generates a host of favorable resultant benefits, including increased feelings of well-being and flows of good energy. It also provides one of the most direct means of accessing higher states of awareness.

The key to effective meditation is focusing your thoughts on a single theme or object. (For advanced practitioners, another object of contemplation is focusing on nothing at all.) The end goal of this focused meditation is to venture inward to your own core in order to unleash its potent arsenal of spiritual energy.

The practice is often difficult for many at first. However, stick with it and expect to invest meaningful amounts of time practicing. It takes time to learn how to silence your mind, but once you achieve it, you'll be glad you did. Besides the known spiritual boosts, science has also caught up with the fact that meditation brings tangible benefits. Studies link meditation to improved physical and emotional states as well as feelings of sustained well-being.

Numerous books already exist on how to meditate, so visit your local bookstore to determine which style best suits you. Many find visually based books (such as meditation books utilizing mandalas and labyrinths) to be the best place to start since their format naturally serves toward focusing one's thoughts.

# Walk Every Chance You Get!

*N*ature offers the greatest well of spiritual energy we can experience. I like to label nature my temple because of the spiritual refreshment it provides. In fact, spending time in nature is the best means of fostering feelings of well-being, whether as a seeker of awareness or a general connoisseur of good health.

Nature is able to provide these benefits because its disposition is pure and collaborative. Its design of choice naturally generates symmetry, holism, and balance. It takes only what it needs and no more. What better wisdom by which to live life?

Nature's infinite beauty, nuance, colors, and variety also offer great inspiration. It is no wonder that artists have long considered nature to be their greatest motivator and source of creativity. Nature speaks directly to our mind's natural ability to recognize aesthetics and beauty.

Because her creations exude the universe's wisdom, spending time in nature and studying her forms offers the best means of exposing yourself to her way and more quickly assimilating it. Studying her designs also keeps us mindful of the wonder of being, including the many miracles it takes to animate life and existence.

Her abundance and perfection also speak to our souls, letting us know there's a larger purpose to the universe and our lives.

# Keep a Journal

There's no better way to build a new dialogue with the world—and yourself—than keeping a journal.

Think of your journal as a forest floor. As you write things down, you plant seeds of thought that grow into larger ideas. A journal becomes the living tissue from which ideas can interconnect, overlap, and resonate. Like roots spreading in all directions, your ideas become more robust and more widely considered. They can also bifurcate in new and unexpected directions or at other times, join with the roots of other trees to merge and cross-pollinate into something entirely new.

So start a journal today, and let it help you better discover your world, develop a wider dialogue, interconnect things, and become more aware.

# Stretch Your Mind

*I* believe one of life's goals is to expand our circle of space and knowledge. As infants, we could only see things up close. As children, we were only able to see a few meters about us. Later, our circle expanded to the edges of our room and then eventually to include our house and yard. As older kids and then teenagers, we expanded into neighborhoods and possibly even the township in which we lived. In college, we started to stretch across a state, and in our careers across a nation, possibly even traveling across national borders.

But all of this is just the physical aspect. We also need to stretch our imagination. To the peaks of mountaintops we must climb but also into the hearts of atoms and stars we must dive, journeying across oceans, solar systems, and galaxies. Imagine getting your arms around the entire universe and getting to know what resides at its heart.[7]

Stretch your mind without limitation and you will come to know the unimaginable.

# Surround Yourself with Good People

The people around us have a huge influence on our thoughts and moods. We do ourselves great favors by surrounding ourselves with good and positive people. They uplift our mood and inspire us to think expansively, unlike negative and hateful types who only confine and limit us to small spaces.

To help you feel better and think bigger, seek out and surround yourself with good, honest, and thoughtful people. Their smiles, encouragement, and words will boost your spirit and help keep your mind clear to pursue greater things.

# Fill Your Life with Great Things

To ensure that your experience of life and your worldview are as wide and beautiful as they can be, fill your life with the best of everything.

As the best of the best are often far removed from mainstream culture, you'll need to dedicate time to seeking them out. The rewards will be well worth the effort as they open up countless passageways to wonder, knowledge, and pleasurable experience—things such as creative passion, music, philosophy, poetry, literature, inspired science, art, great ideas, religion, and mysticism. They are the heart and soul of man's collective psyche and some of the greatest creations the universe has to offer.

Also seek out—and express at every possible moment—humanity's greatest expressions of kindness, love, gratitude, integrity, sincerity, and goodness. Each time you do so, you will place yourself in proximity to the divine and thereby fill your soul with more of its magic.

# Take Time for Yourself

It's nearly impossible to ascend mountaintops or journey inward to your heart if you're continually distracted by others and pop culture. To arrive at new and enlightening destinations, you'll need to take quiet time for yourself.

Sharing and being with others is one of life's greatest joys. However, it also keeps us from getting to know ourselves better and from growing. This doesn't mean you need to become a hermit, but it does mean that you will need to dedicate more time to yourself. To achieve this, make it a point to find quiet spaces and time just for yourself. Stop at a park on the way home and take a walk. Sit in a coffee shop and take notes or read a great novel. The same goes for your interactions with pop culture. If you are continually engaged in the negativity of news and the competition culture, your mind will never find the time to stretch and relax.

To attain higher states of awareness, it's recommended that you largely limit your ties to 'the machine'. Turn off and walk away from television and the ridiculous hype and expectations it creates. Keep the competition culture at bay by drastically reducing your viewing of sports and competition TV, such as the endless stream of reality-based shows. Fill all your newfound time with more meaningful pursuits such as art, books, and walks in nature. Make more time for yourself and you will begin to grow again.

# Koans Can Hasten the Change

To foster the conditions of sudden enlightenment, Rinzai Zen, a sect of Zen in Japanese Buddhism, implements a method known as *satori* whereby masters (called *Sanzen*) have students contemplate *koan* paradoxes followed by a surprise act to push the student into an awakening experience.

The process goes like this: the Sanzen challenges the student to solve a koan followed by long periods of intense meditation coupled with periodic reviews of the student's view on the koan. Sensing when the student has reached the verge of sudden enlightenment, an experienced master will shock him or her into the satori experience with an unexpected act, such as a blow with a stick or a loud yell.

I often wonder if my journey shares parallels to the koan experience—increasingly deep contemplations (calderas, milky ways, big bangs), all leading up to a sudden shock (a relocation around the world and various personal struggles).

As it relates to your journey, take up some meaningful koan contemplations and later look for sources or hints to a sudden surprise that might push you into your own satori experience.

# Every Experience, a Chance to Center and Grow

*E*very moment, every experience is a divine opportunity to center.

Everything is here for a reason. It has an origin, past, secret, and mystery to solve. A tree started as a seedling. Ongoing arguments in our lives started and continue because the originating disagreement remains unresolved. Entire philosophies begin with the thoughts of a single man.

By traversing the path to the center of all things, you will find its purpose, meaning, and reason for being here. You will come to better understand your world, the mind of the Great Creator, and yourself.

Use the following excerpt from *The Centerpath Chronicles*[8] to bring this concept into your heart:

All of life is a mystery moving toward hidden centers. Once you arrive at the center, the journey is complete; we have found what we are looking for: the essence, source, and reason why.

All things enduring and meaningful are tied to this process. Arguments, fights and battles. The outcomes of hunts, the preparation of meals, and musical and sensual climaxes. Shaman rituals, births, hugs, cries, and deaths.

Upon arriving, we discover the journey's secret. While always surprising, it's also always comprised of the same stuff: beauty, truth, and essence.

All of the universe is destined to create a crescendo to a center and crash back down on the shore where it began.

All of life and its experiences are journeys back to the source. All experiences are moments of creation. They produce a center and thus set a future trap for us to be drawn and return to. The larger whole is cast.

All the mind's structures are intended to find those traps, to traverse a meaningful journey to that place. The reason and essence lying in wait.

See the splendor of centers—moments of truth, love, beauty, brightness, and complexity. Experience the journey to secrets, hearts of the matter, and where the truth lay in hiding.

Rejoice in being a center—a glowing heart. Its penultimate power is the universe's greatest stuff—beauty, truth, essence, love, compassion. This is being true to the way of things, yourself, and the universe.

Rejoice in the journey of being. Traversing to the essence of all your experiences. Once your new habit becomes latched to the larger branch of the apple tree, the journey gets steeper and sweeter. Who's waiting for you at the end of it makes its strenuous ascent infinitely worth it.

Rejoice in experiencing all of nature's stunningly beautiful creations. All were carved out by things seeking their very own, consistently patterned, center-oriented destiny.

In Centerpath, we traverse many journeys to the heart of things in order to gain unique insights, great perspectives, and valuable trinkets of wisdom. Hopefully its many nuggets of insight will fascinate and inspire you on the way to your very own Centerpath destination.

# Get Closer to the Source

*A* great means of uplifting your life—and possibly hastening your awakening—is getting closer to the source of all things. After all, what's more inspiring than being up close to the universe's greatest treasures?

To begin reaping benefits from the source, you'll need to get closer to heavenly things. What and where are these divine sources, you ask? They are the Great Creator's very creations!

Although recognizing heaven's enchanted artwork might be difficult at first, there is a means to jumpstart the process. For while all of nature's creations possess strong shades of divine perfection, they are not all created equally. Some glow more brilliantly than all others; there are diamonds in the rough and beacons capable of guiding us more directly to nature's rich enchantment.

Where are these priceless charms located? Mostly everywhere about you—in the heart and soul of nature's most dazzling creations. They are in the brilliant radiance of flowers, rainbows and sunsets, a sparkling glacier, temples, and infinite stars on a moonless night. They are in crystals, a mother's patience, waterfalls, mountain vistas, Van Gogh's skies, and the bliss of a child's smile. They are in the words of Whitman, Goethe, Lao Zhu, and many other great minds and artists. They are where truth, meaning, and purpose reside. They are God's smile shining brightly through her brightest creations.

Experiencing the divine becoming your new day-to-day passion. Seek out powerful things, places, people, and spaces. Extract beauty from the heart of all things—one small yet immense encounter at a time. Fill your life, and your experience of it, ever more with the finest the universe has to offer. Each occurrence brings you one step closer to the soul of the universe. Exercised faithfully, it brings us to enriched and elated states of being, placing us closer to God's replenishing splendor than we ever imagined possible.

# Give Thanks to the Source

Though once an integral part of our lives, the offering of thanks and gratitude seems to have fallen out of favor these days. I believe this fundamental shift in behavior has resulted from our living in an age where convenience reigns. Because it seems that we can get whatever we want with relatively little effort and no apparent causality, we tend to take the view—and extremely simplistically so, I might add—of, "Why do we need to give thanks and *to whom*?"

However, the ritual of giving thanks is as valid as ever and brings with it very real and tangible benefits. Moreover, due to the fragile state of the human condition these days, giving thanks may be more important than ever.

The first benefit arising from giving thanks is that it keeps us closer to those things that are most vital and therefore most meaningful to our well-being. Family and the earthly resources we consume are quintessential to our survival. Being closer to them both physically, and in heart and mind brings us back to the spirit of our being—indeed closer to the Great Creator. Remaining closer to what brings us pleasure, happiness, and indeed life itself, our lives become enchanted—energized by the life force running throughout all things.

Giving thanks to the fountainheads of our lives also puts things in broader perspective. The sources of our existence are ground zeroes—all of our lives originate and emanate from them. Reconnecting with the place where all things begin reacquaints us with the full range of experience. From ground and air to sea and sky, and in plants and animals— from home and shelter to food and the love of family, regrounding ourselves to the bedrocks of being brings the full range of life, our experience of it, and nature's bounty into sharper focus.

Furthermore, our minds naturally recognize the exceeding importance of things closest to our core—and reward us when we express gratitude for them. In his book, *Born to Be Good: The Science of a Meaningful Life,*[9] Dacher Keltner outlines how deeply rooted portions of our minds are hardwired to take note of and reward us (via the release of good-feeling mental drugs) when we give thanks. The very act itself improves our well-being and progressively reinforces what's truly meaningful in our lives.

So don't be afraid to give thanks frequently and copiously, to food, bountifulness, existence, nature, good fortune, loved ones, successes, and career. By doing so, you'll shake the tree of good fortune and release its plentiful payload in ways both seen and unseen, lifting yourself, others, and the rest of the universe to a higher plane of existence.

# How Will You Know You're There?

*Y*ou'll know you're there when you feel everything has changed in a new and wonderful way. You'll revel in tumbling down bunny-hole after bunny-hole in search of deeper truths and understanding. You'll see nature in a completely different light. Instead of viewing her with indifference or as simply something to consume (as society teaches us to do), you'll view her with awe and respect, as the provider for all we have and the ultimate source of wisdom and inspiration.

You will see man's world in a different light, no longer separate from nature but as an extension of her. Your definition of who and what is great will be redefined. You'll recognize society's leaders (bankers, CEOs, politicians, and entrepreneurs) for what they are—groups of socially talented

*Jin Nua*

and intelligent people who nevertheless lack deep knowledge and true wisdom.

Your focus will also shift from a life rooted in media and history to appreciating true inspiration and greatness.

You will be drawn to the truly inspired and enduring—a legion formed mostly of great thinkers, philosophers, spiritual and religious leaders, artists, and musicians.

# What to Expect

*E*xpect everything to change.

Expect excitement, wonder, and awe to reenter your life.

Expect your sensory sensitivity to increase greatly (especially to visual and audible stimuli). For me personally, the vividness of colors and sounds became exceptionally acute.

Expect your ability to focus on an item or subject to become significantly enhanced. You'll be able to consider concepts deeply at practically any moment, whether on a bus, waiting in line, or walking (some might call it walking meditation).

You won't be afraid to take on any subject—no matter how big or small. You'll take pleasure in trying to understand the cosmos, humanity, and the greatest scientific and philosophical ideas.

Expect a reprogramming of your belief systems. Similar to sages describing the experience as the bottom falling out of the bucket, you'll find that once your bucket empties itself, you'll have the opportunity to rebuild an entirely new worldview.

Having reconnected to the center of your being, you will become more streamlined. Becoming less dependent on existing beliefs telling you how things are, you will begin taking in things as they simply are. Your objectivity will increase dramatically.

You'll come to realize that you don't know everything (and in fact you can't ever know everything, especially as it relates to the essence of existence and being). Surprisingly, you'll quickly come to realize that this is a strength. This is a dramatic change from what others are (and you used to be) accustomed to (i.e., our disposition is to shun uncertainty in lieu of certainties). You'll realize absolute sureness doesn't exist anywhere and believing in certainties in fact limits our capability to think freely and expansively.

You'll become increasingly uninterested in the agendas of the rat race and media. You'll recognize that practically all beliefs and opinions are merely reflections of the messages broadcast by the media and that most individuals speak and act in concert with what they see and hear from these manipulating outlets.

Allow your creativity to explode. Developing your own ideas, music, and art will no longer be foreign to you. You will think in much wider and broader scales. You will be able to conceptualize and articulate ideas far beyond your current capabilities. You will come to love the feelings of bliss associated with new realizations and epiphanies.

Expect difficulty in communicating your new ideas and enthusiasm with others. Others need to stay relatively near their current belief systems (which, as you'll soon see, are largely the same across all peoples). Peddle your ideas lightly to avoid arousing feelings of uncertainty in others or giving them the impression that you are being elusive or arrogant.

# What Should You Do?

*W*hat should you do when you enter the realm of awareness? Everything you can! Don't waste a moment! Explore, absorb, and expose yourself to everything and anything you can. Mostly, just follow what interests and inspires you at the time. You'll be surprised by just how naturally it comes to you.

Some additional advice:

- Take walks.
- Write down all your thoughts. Keep a journal.
- Don't throw your journals away, and make sure to date them. They're a great record of your real-time observations and just as importantly, of why you felt the way you did at any particular time.
- Listen to new types of music. Be sure to include classic and jazz in your new repertoire.

- Listen to (and record on your phone) the music in your head.

- Buy great books. And find the time to read them.

- Buy books on biology, astronomy, cosmology, spiritualism, mysticism, poetry, new science, old science—anything that interests you.

- Buy a lot of image-based books.

- Travel.

- Visit art museums.

- Spend a lot of time in libraries.

- Buy a whiteboard to help visualize and interconnect your thoughts.

- Take up new pursuits:

  o Get an eight-track recorder and make music.

  o Buy a piano, guitar, or drum set.

  o Take up painting.

  o Shoot a lot of pictures.

  o Write poetry, a book, or a movie.

# *Does It Change over Time?*

*M*ost people report the first two to three years of their newfound awareness as being the most intense in terms of focus, sheer delight, and elated experience. Don't fret. Your newfound assets will remain strong for years to come. However, do keep in mind that the first few years hold the most space to create, grow new ideas, and roam wildly about the terrain of being. Don't waste a moment!

Walk continuously in nature, and dive deeply into as much great art, music, and literature as you can possibly take in! Read copious amounts of books on spiritualism, mysticism, mandalas, chaos theory, fractal science, and the like.

In this period, be sure to keep a journal (and store them properly!). Make sure that you date the pages of your journal to help you track your progress (and especially to help you sort your notes when you revisit them years hence).

# Your Journey

No one knows his or her path or where life will ultimately lead us. Will our journey lead to a successful career, a great work of art, a beautiful family, our destiny, or an awakening? No matter where it leads, you can help ensure that it will be abundant and that you leave behind a positive legacy if you follow the general recommendations included in this book.

So get busy! Walk in nature. Slow your life and take up meditation. Surround yourself with great people. Take in quality art, literature, and music. Get closer to the source. Take better care of yourself. Experience grand things and ideas. Listen to and follow your heart. By doing so, you will have elevated your bittersweet time on this planet to levels of delight unimaginable.

More than just improving your life and the lives of those around you, every time you act mindfully and meaningfully, you will have contributed to a better universe and reconnected with the divine in ways you never even dreamed possible.

# Bibliography

1    Fischer-Schreiber, Ingrid; Ehrhard, Franz-Karl; Diener, Michael S. (2008), Lexicon Boeddhisme. Wijsbegeerte, religie, psychologie, mystiek, cultuur an literatuur, Asoka, p.50.

2    Park, Sung-bae (1983), Buddhist Faith and Sudden Enlightenment, SUNY Press, p.127.

3    Lusthaus, Dan (1998), Buddhist Philosophy, Chinese. In: Routledge Encyclopedia of Philosophy: Index, Taylor & Francis.

4    Mäll, Linnart (2005), Studies in the Aṣṭasāhasrikā Prajñāpāramitā and other essays, Motilal Banarsidass Publishers, p. 83.

5    This isn't all bad. We indeed need to learn appropriate means of interacting in larger social circles; it's just that modern socialization is highly lopsided to favor society's agenda (that there's only value in winning, competitiveness, history, wars, etc.) and teaches little to nothing on holistic and balanced approaches to life.

6    Jin Nua, *Heart of the Universe* (Centerpath Book Publishing LLC, 2013).

[7] See Jin Nua, *Heart of the Universe* (Centerpath Book Publishing LLC, 2013) to help you find that heart.

[8] Jin Nua, *The Centerpath Chronicles* (Centerpath Book Publishing LLC, 2013), p. 74.

[9] Dacher Keltner, *Born to Be Good: The Science of a Meaningful Life* (New York: W.W. Norton & Co, 2009).

Printed in the United States
By Bookmasters